ISBN: 978-108789320-4

Published by Cypress Hills Press
Brooklyn, New York

Book design: Richard Tackett
http://www.richtackett.com

CRIBB:
THE SERIES

BY

SCOTT V. PALMER

INTRODUCTION

This is a reference book about the television series *Cribb* which ran for 14 episodes from 1979-1981. It was made by Granada Television. The book includes the 14 episodes in date order, and includes complete cast lists, numerous photographs, a story synopsis, directorial credits, and original dates of transmission.

The series was based on books written by Peter Lovesey, set in Victorian London, and starring Alan Dobie as Detective Sergeant Cribb of Scotland Yard. William Simon also appeared as Constable Thackeray, as well as David Waller as Chief Inspector Jowett.

The series portrayed life in Victorian England, and the episodes included many true historical events such as the publication of Three Men in a Boat as well as the sale of Jumbo, the London Zoo's famous elephant, who was bought by the Barnum & Bailey circus.

Cribb came from humble beginnings and was no-nonsense in his approach. This often put him at odds with Chief Inspector Jowett, a social climber with many well-to-do connections.

The stories are inventive and different as regards theme and location. Costumes, locations, references to contemporary events and efforts to create a correct period atmosphere, language and manners suggest that the writer and the production team went to great pains to achieve authenticity. It also has quality guest stars, good value, enjoyable and intelligent.

TABLE OF CONTENTS

WAXWORK EPISODE 1

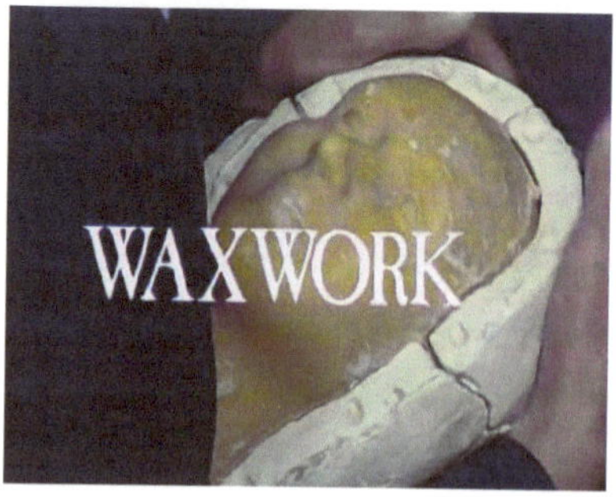

DIRECTED BY June Wyndham-Davies
ORIGINAL AIR DATE: December 23, 1979

CAST

Alan Dobie.......Detective Sergeant Cribb
David Waller.........Chief Inspector Jowett
Carol Royle.....................Miriam Cromer
Gerald Sim................Inspector Waterlow
Laurence Payne..............Howard Cromer
Bernard Archard....Governor of Newgate
Elspeth March...........Dorothea Davenant
Roy Evans.............................Shopkeeper
David Ashford..............Simon Allingham
John Quarmby................Inspector Moser
James Warrior.......................James Berry
William Abney.................Joseph Tussaud
Ernest Hare...............Mr. Justice Colbeck
Elizabeth Burger...............................Bell
Barbara Bolton...........................Hawkins
Susie Blake............................Lottie Piper
Ursula Mohan........................Sarah Berry
Stuart Latham.....................Prison Doctor
Paul Williamson....................Headmaster
Peter Mackriel................Wallis the Clerk
Jacob Witkin...............................Brodski
Geoffrey Larder...............Josiah Perceval
Joanne Zorian................Judith Honeycutt

Alan Dobie

David Waller

Carol Royle

Gerald Sim

Laurence Payne

Bernard Archard

Elspeth March

Roy Evans

Lesley Nightingale............................Maid
Alick Hayes.................Clerk of the Court
Mark Hudson..............................Call Boy

David Ashford

John Quarmby

James Warrior

William Abney

Ernest Hare

Elizabeth Burger

Barbara Bolton

Susie Blake

Ursula Mohan

Stuart Latham

Paul Williamson

Peter Mackriel

Jacob Witkin

Geoffrey Larder

Joanne Zorian

Lesley Nightingale

Alick Hayes

Mark Hudson

Doctor

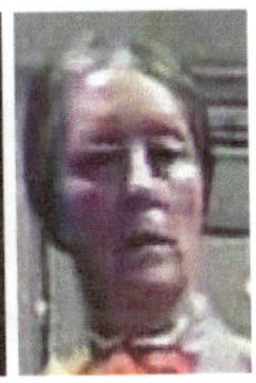
Dresser

1888: Miriam Cromer, wife of society photographer Howard Cromer, confesses to poisoning her husband's assistant, Josiah Percival, who was blackmailing her over photographs for which she posed years earlier.

Paul Williamson, Alan Dobie

James Warrior, William Abney

She is to be hanged, and her likeness immortalized at Madame Tussaud's waxworks, as is that of the hangman, James Berry. Inspector Jowett believes there is doubt as to her guilt.

A wave of public sympathy is forcing the Home Secretary to wonder if clemency should be granted. As it appears that she could not have had access to the poison cabinet, Chief Inspector Jowett asks Sergeant Cribb to investigate. He begins by establishing that her husband's alibi is not perfect.

Carol Royle, James Warrior

Laurence Payne, Alan Dobie

Cribb interviews Inspector Waterlow, who made the arrest. The Inspector is going to retire soon, and admits that as Mrs. Cromer confessed he saw no reason to fully investigate every aspect of the case.

Alan Dobie, Laurence Payne

Carol Royle, Barbara Bolton

Gerals Sim looks through the carnations

Elizabeth Burger, Carol Royle, Barbara Bolton

Ursula Mohan, James Warrior

Alan Dobie as Sergeant Cribb

Cribb finds that a close family friend, solicitor Simon Allingham, seems to know more than he is saying regarding the behavior of the deceased, Miriam, and Howard. He agrees with most people's low opinion of the deceased.

Cribb also attempts to track down the other girls who posed with her in the rude photographs. One, Judith Honeycutt, died of the same poison that killed Percival.

Barbara Bolton, Stuart Latham

Television Poster

Bernard Archard with the confession

David Waller, Alan Dobie

Chief Inspector Jowett celebrates the solution

Alan Dobie gives his comments

Another girl, actress Lottie Piper, girlfriend of the deceased (and the only person that seems to have anything good to say about him), tells Cribb that the photographer who took the photos had an affair with Judith, disappearing after her death.

Cribb believes that that photographer is Miriam's husband who killed Judith and who is now on the run. Has he framed Miriam or is she keeping quiet to protect her husband? Or has a clever plot been arranged between husband and wife for some other purpose?

Alick Hayes, Ernest Hare

Bernard Archard, David Ashford

David Waller, Alan Dobie

Miriam and the doctor

Visiting Miriam in her cell along with the prison governor, solicitor Simon Allingham, and Chief Inspector Jowett, Cribb begins interrogating Miriam-who thinks that a pardon will be issued for her-especially when she says her husband killed Perceval.

Unfortunately, Miriam can't keep her mouth shut; Cribb says she should have taken Allingham's advice and said nothing. Howard Cromer had an alibi-he was in Allingham's office when Perceval was poisoned.

That leaves only Miriam; Cribb tells Jowett that Miriam, he believes, also killed Judith Honeycutt, in order to marry Howard. At the appointed time, Miriam is executed; her likeness is seen along with hangman James Berry in Madame Tussaud's.

Roy Evans, Alan Dobie

Alan Dobie, Peter Mackriel

SWING, SWING TOGETHER EPISODE 2

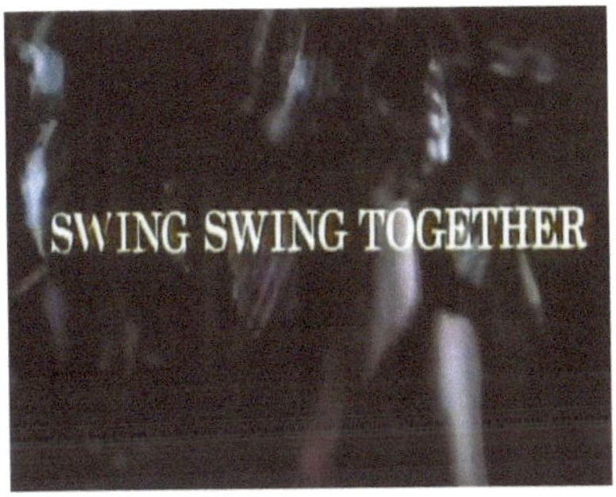

DIRECTED BY June Wyndham-Davies
ORIGINAL AIR DATE: April 13, 1980

CAST

Alan Dobie.......Detective Sergeant Cribb
William Simons......Constable Thackeray
Ronald Lacey......................Percy Bustard
Heather Moray......................Harriet Shaw
Albert Welling..............Constable Hardy
Brian Rawlinson....................Jim Hackett
Mark Burns......................John Fernandez
Jane How.................Melanie Bonner-Hill
Ronald Russell....................Fernandez Sr.
Sheila Keith.......................Miss Plummer
Michael Ripper....................Lock Keeper
Bill Shine.................................Landlord
Robert Fyffe................................Lucifer
Peter Birrel.......................................Gold
Debbie Farrington..........................Molly
Victoria Burton.................................Jane
Myles Hoyle.........................Humberstone
John Grillo...............................Goldstein
Carole Hayman...............................Dinah
Richard Goolden..........................Warden
Nigel Bowden.......River Bank Constable
Steven Mann................Oxford Constable
Alan Norburn...........Scotland Yard Clerk

Alan Dobie

William Simons

Ronald Lacey

Heather Moray

Albert Welling

Brian Rawlinson

Mark Burns

Jane How

Ronald Russell

Sheila Keith

Michael Ripper

Bill Shine

Robert Fyffe

Peter Birrel

Debbie Farrington

Victoria Burton

Myles Hoyle

John Grillo

Carole Hayman

Richard Goolden

Nigel Bowden

Steven Mann

Alan Norburn

Desk Sergeant

Dog

When Harriet Smith and two other lady students from the Elfrida Teacher Training College go for a midnight dip in the river they do not expect to see a corpse being dumped over the side of a boat.

Heather Moray, Ronald Lacey

After Harriet has informed the authorities Cribb and Thackeray are sent, undercover, as boating tourists, which Thackeray, who keeps falling overboard, detests.

Albert Welling, William Simons

Alan Dobie, Myles Hoyle

Bill Shine, William Simons

William Simons, Albert Welling

Myles Hoyle smoking his pipe

At the morgue, a man's body has come in. Cribb, Thackeray, and Constable Hardy examine it; Cribb notices the corpse has a dog bite on the leg.

There is no shortage of suspects; many men were in the area at the time, including a trio of Londoners re-tracing the journey of the 'Three Men In A Boat,' the successful new comic novel.

Heather Moray, Peter Birrel, William Simons

Heather Moray, Alan Dobie

Heather Moray, Albert Welling

SWING, SWING
TOGETHER
A SERGEANT CRIBB ADVENTURE
AS FEATURED ON GRANADA T.V.

TV Poster

Also on hand is an Oxford professor whose uncle is a local prison governor, and two convicts who have just escaped from his prison. Then, another body is discovered.

Heather Moray and Alan Dobie

Heather Moray, Alan Dobie

Television Poster

Heather Moray, William Simons

Heather Moray, William Simons, Alan Dobie

It's a man, also in the river. Identification says he is a Mr. Bonner-Hill, from Oxford. Cribb thinks he was killed in mistake for someone else. It turns out, as Cribb suspects, the victim was killed because the killers thought he was Jack the Ripper.

ABRACADAVER EPISODE 3

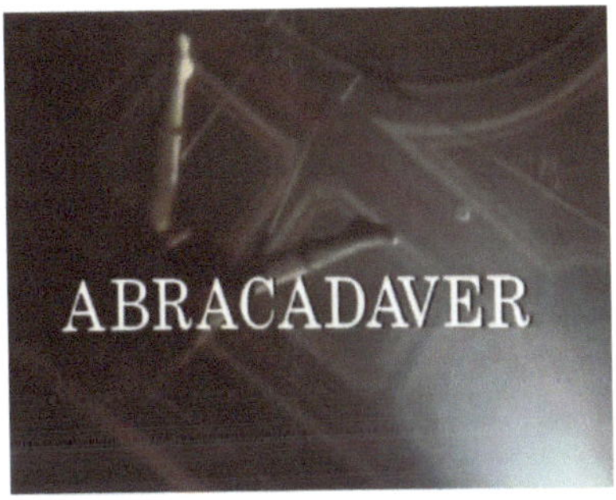

DIRECTED BY Julian Amyes
ORIGINAL AIR DATE: April 20, 1980

CAST

Alan Dobie.......Detective Sergeant Cribb
William Simons......Constable Thackeray
David Waller........Chief Inspector Jowett
Patsy Rowlands.......................Mrs. Body
Julia Chambers......................Ellen Blake
Ian Collier....................................Albert
Peter Bland.....................Samuel Plunkett
Peggy Ann Clifford.........Albert's Mother
Anthony Pedley....................Major Chick
Chubby Oates..........................Chairman
Jerold Wells...........................Manservant
Wendy Holloway..................Lola Pinkus
Valerie Holloway.................Bella Pinkus
Derek Tansley.......................Buckmaster
Billy Wild........................Knife Thrower
Robert Kingswell.......................P.C. Salt
Jeffrey Longmore..................P.C. Battree
Peter Newton..........................Bert Smee
Stuart Teale.........................George Smee
Richard Merson......................Sam Fagan
Harry Beety......................Stage Manager
Stromboli...Virgo
Kate Lee...............................Promenader

Alan Dobie

William Simons

David Waller

Patsy Rowlands

Julia Chambers

Ian Collier

Peter Bland

Peggy Ann Clifford

Candace Hartley..................Girl With Flat

Anthony Pedley

Chubby Oates

Jerold Wells

Wendy Holloway

Valerie Holloway

Derek Tansley

Billy Wild

Richard Merson

Harry Beety

Kate Lee

Entetrtainer

A practical joker is deliberately ruining acts at London music-halls, with his pranks ranging from the mildly embarrassing to downright dangerous.

Julia Chambers, William Simons, Alan Dobie

Coach rolling through the fog

Patsy Rowlands, Alan Dobie

Cribb comments to Constable Thackeray that there have been seven accidents in music halls during the last four weeks. When Cribb gets a note telling him that an accident is about to happen, he and Thackeray head to the music hall.

One of the performers, Albert, is bitten by a dog-who had been replaced in the act by a more vicious canine. Cribb's investigations lead to activities which certain people are keen to keep secret.

Anthony Pedley taking notes

Alan Dobie, Jerold Wells

Peter Bland as Samuel Plunkett

David Waller as Jowett

During one of the performances, Cribb and Thackeray are on hand when a woman, Lola Pinkus, is murdered. Cribb deduces she was poisoned with prussic acid.

Alan Dobie, William Simons

Alan Dobie and Effigy

William Simons, Alan Dobie

Billy Wild throwing knives

William Simons, Alan Dobie, David Waller

Back at Scotland Yard, Cribb and Thackeray report their findings to Chief Inspector Jowett. They also say the naked women parading in front of eminent members of society were indecent. Jowett says they are being prudes.

When singer Ellen Blake goes missing, her father receives a letter saying she has been kidnapped. After Ellen turns up safe, Cribb reveals there was no kidnapping-Ellen arranged it all. She also killed Lola.

William Simons, Alan Dobie

Ian Collier, Peter Bland

Cribb and Thackeray in fancy dress

THE DETECTIVE WORE SILK DRAWERS EPISODE 4

DIRECTED BY Alan Grint

ORIGINAL AIR DATE: April 27, 1980

CAST

Alan Dobie.......Detective Sergeant Cribb
David Waller.........Chief Inspector Jowett
William Simons......Constable Thackeray
Barry Andrews......Constable Henry Jago
Norma West.........................Isabel Vibart
David Hargreaves............Robert D'Estin
Mark Eden.......................Edmund Vibart
Jimmy Gardner...........................Boatman
Alf Joint.......................................The Ox
David Rhule............................The Ebony
Alfie Curtis..........................Matt Beckett
Mavis Blake......................Lydia Boltover
Campbell O'Brien......................Landlord
Dave Thomas................................Cabby
Hannah Jowett.......................Girl in Pub
Les Clark, Derek Ware..............Referees

Alan Dobie

David Waller

William Simons

Barry Andrews

Norma West

David Hargreaves

Mark Eden

Jimmy Gardner

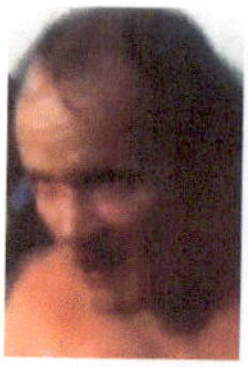
Alf Joint

David Rhule

Alfie Curtis

Mavis Blake

Dave Thomas

Hannah Jowett

Les Clark

Derek Ware

Boxing Fan 1

Boxing Fan 2

Boxing Fan 3

When headless male corpses are found floating in the river the common link is scarred hands, which points to them having taken part in illegal bare-knuckle boxing.

David Waller as Chief Inspector Jowett

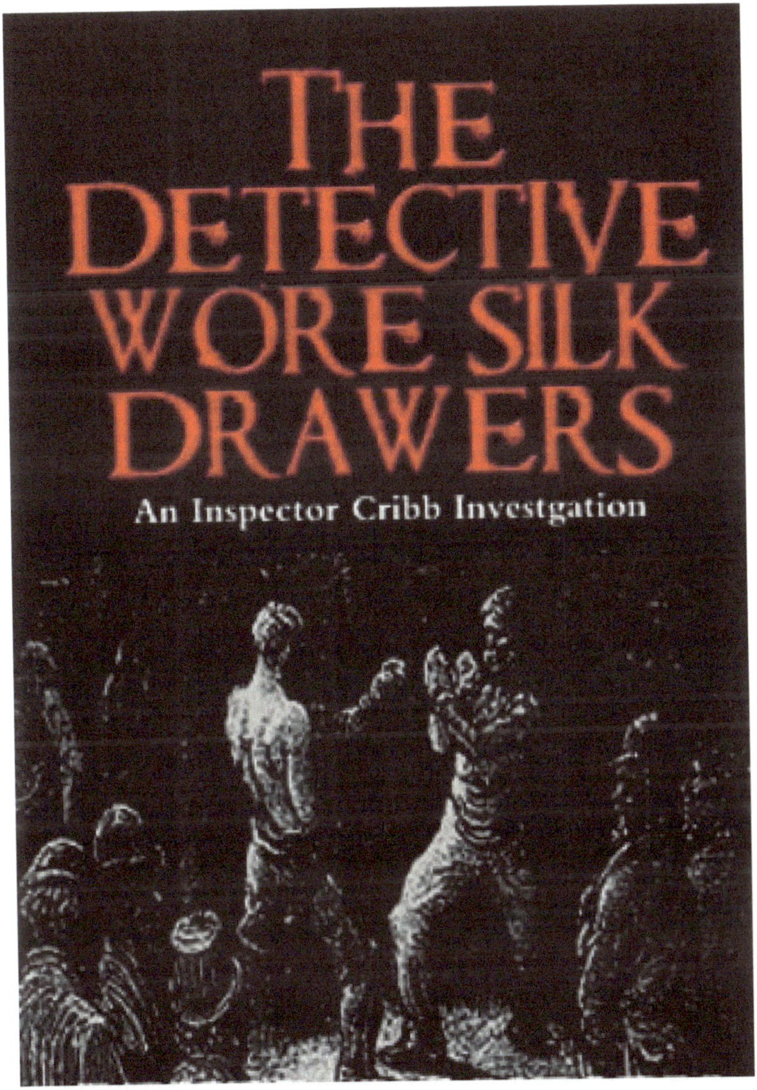

TV Poster

Strapping Constable Jago, the force's amateur boxing champion, poses as a boxer in search of a prize fight with Cribb as his manager. This leads to the alluring Mrs. Vibart.

Cribb suspects that the headless boxers were not local men, as there had been nobody reported missing. So Cribb and Thackery head to Mrs. Vibart's large estate.

William Simons, Barry Andrews, Alan Dobie

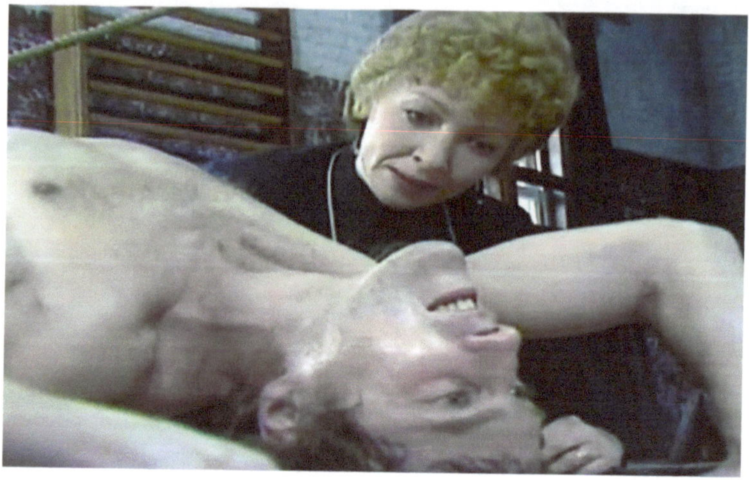

Norma West, Barry Andrews

David Hargreaves, David Rhule

View of the lake

They learn she has a number of fighters, and also controls the fights, determining how many rounds they should last and which fighter should win.

Jago, who has joined her stable of boxers, is now living at the house. Cribb tells Jowett just what's going on; Jowett cuts him quite a bit of slck in the investigation.

Alan Dobie, William Simons

Mark Eden, David Hargreaves

David Hargreaves, Mark Eden

Alan Dobie, Jimmy Gardner

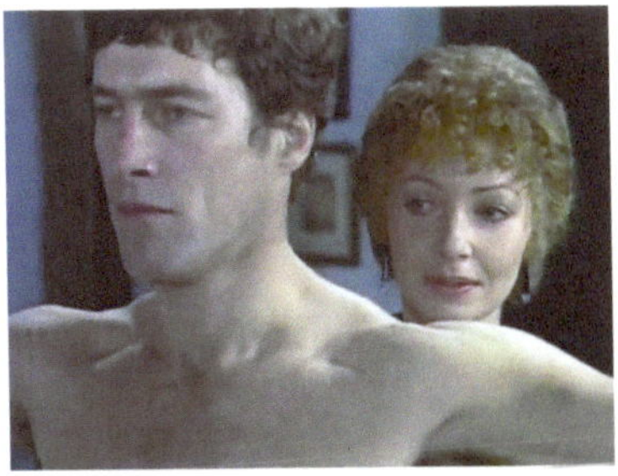

Barry Andrews, Norma West

Alan Dobie as Sergeant Cribb

When Mrs. Vibart is murdered, Jago becomes a prime suspect. Cribb has to clear his name before he takes too many beatings in the ring. When Jago fights The Ebony, Cribb and Thackeray head for the bout.

Jago takes quite a beating, being knocked out after 22 rounds, just as Cribb arrives. Cribb interviews all the suspects; through a ruse involving a gun, Cribb gets a confession from the killer. Jago is promoted to sergeant.

Alan Dobie, David Waller

William Simons, Mavis Blake

Alan Dobie, William Simons

THE HORIZONTAL WITNESS EPISODE 5

DIRECTED BY Alan Grint
ORIGINAL AIR DATE: May 4, 1980

CAST

Alan Dobie.......Detective Sergeant Cribb
David Waller.........Chief Inspector Jowett
William Simons......Constable Thackeray
John Ringham............James Hepplewhite
Norman Jones........................Joe Calhoun
James Coyle.....................Charles Vokins
Elizabeth Bennett..........Sister Armstrong
Jennifer Guy.................................Flossie
Linda Robson................Bessie Hardicker
Molly Veness.....................................Peg
Jean Warren....................................Alice
June Page............................Lady Alcock
Steve Fletcher............................Bootboy
Mark Bond.........................Young Client
John Cannon, Eric Kent..............Roughs
Russell Denton, Alick Hayes...Customers

Alan Dobie

David Waller

William Simons

John Ringham

Norman Jones

James Coyle

Elizabeth Bennett

Jennifer Guy

Molly Veness

Jean Warren

Steve Fletcher

Mark Bond

John Cannon

Eric Kent

Bootboy

Club Member

Minister

Mourner 1

Mourner 2

Mourner 3

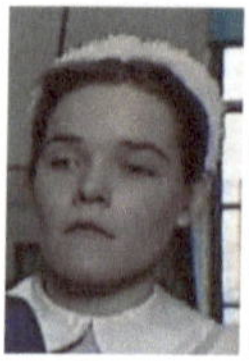
Nurse 1

Nurse 2

Nurse 3

Patient 1

Patient 2

Student 1

Student 2

Student 3

Fred Calhoun, a key player in London's vice world, is found dead in one of his own brothels. Unreliable witness Charlie Vokins, who had a score to settle with him, claims to know the murderer but wants to make a deal with the police.

John Ringham, David Waller

David Waller, Alan Dobie

As well as the deceased's brother Joe, the other major suspect is Dr. Hepplewhite who owed gaming debts to the dead man. Thackeray is due to have an operation and Cribb arranges for him to be admitted to the same hospital where Charlie Vokins was taken to recuperate from a severe beating.

James Coyle, Alan Dobie

Fred Calhoun dead on the floor

David Waller, Norman Jones

Elizabeth Bennett, John Ringham

William Simons makes a point

Dr. Hepplewhite therefore becomes the surgeon due to operate on Thackeray and Cribb is anxious to keep his constable safe, particularly as he is a bad patient, constantly exasperating the Matron, Sister Armstrong who is secretly in love with the surgeon.

Cribb visits Thackeray in hospital; it seems that Vokins is in the next bed. Cribb tells the Constable to keep as sharp eye on Vokins, as someone may try to silence him there in the hospital.

Alan Dobie, David Waller

Norman Jones, John Ringham

And as usual, Cribb is right; Calhoun sends a couple of his thugs to the hospital, but they can't get near Vokins, thanks to the watchfulness of Constable Thackeray.

Mourners at the funeral

William Simons playing cards

Eric Kent, John Cannon

Elizabeth Bennett and staff

When Vokins is released, he meets with Cribb and Jowett in the hospital, naming Joe Calhoun as the killer. But Cribb- who knows Vokins was backmailing Dr. Hepplewhite-also knows Calhoun was on the other side of town when the murder was committed.

That leaves only Vokins as the killer; he tries to hold Thackeray as a hostage, but Sister Armstrong stabs him with a hatpin Flossie gave her, and Vokins is apprehended and taken away.

Alan Dobie, David Waller

Eric Kent, John Cannon

WOBBLE TO DEATH EPISODE 6

DIRECTED BY Gordon Flemyng
ORIGINAL AIR DATE: May 11, 1980

CAST

Alan Dobie.......Detective Sergeant Cribb
William Simons......Constable Thackeray
Michael Elphick....................Sol Herriott
Kenneth Cranham....Francis Mostyn-Smith
Andrew Burt................Erskine Chadwick
Jeremy Young........................Peter Chalk
Robert Austin.................Walter Jacobson
Bobbie Brown......................Cora Darrell
Archie Tew.......................Charles Darrell
Ray Jewers..............................Sam Monk
Patrick Waldron...........Fergus O'Flaherty
Paul Barber....................George Williams
Alex Johnston...............................Harvey
Paul Ridley..................................Pincher

Alan Dobie

William Simons

Michael Elphick

Kenneth Cranham

Andrew Burt

Jeremy Young

Robert Austin

Bobbie Brown

Archie Tew

Ray Jewers

Patrick Waldron

Paul Barber

Alex Johnston Paul Ridley

The Pedestrian Championship of the World is taking place in London, an indoor marathon lasting six days and the winner is the man who can be shown to have walked the greatest distance in that time in a style known as wobbling.

Alan Dobie, Kenneth Cranham

The Pedestrian World Championship

Sergeant Cribb placing a bet

Announcement of the race

Favourites are gentleman contender Captain Erskine Chadwick and professional athlete Charlie Darrell. The race begins Monday, November 18, 1879, at 1:00 a.m..

When Darrell collapses, what first appears to have been a cramp proves to be murder. He was poisoned, and later his trainer is also found dead. Thackeray wonders what he and Cribb are doing there; Cribb says the last race ended in a riot.

Robert Austin, Michael Elphick

Alan Dobie, William Simons

Ray Jewers, Bobbie Brown

Robert Austin by the list of entrants

At first it looks like Darrell committed suicide, but Cribb believes otherwise. He suspects Mrs. Darrell, Chadwick, and all the other race entrants.

Cribb agrees that the marathon should be allowed to continue, providing him literally with a race against time to find the murderer. When it's over, Cribb has his man. He also correctly deduced the murder had nothing to do with the race.

Michael Elphick, Alan Dobie

William Simons, Robert Austin

Playing for the festivities

Alan Dobie, William Simons

Alan Dobie as Sergeant Cribb

The race is won by Captain Erskine Chadwick, having completed 538 miles. He receives a cash prize of £500, along with the silver belt. Cribb also had a wager on the winner, for ten pounds.

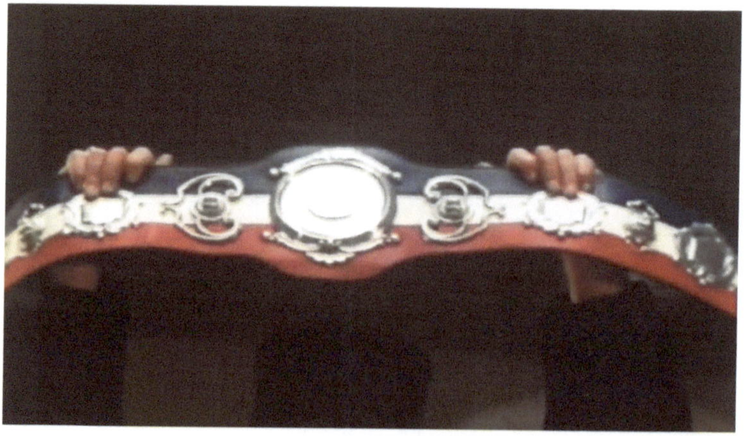

Belt awarded to the winner

Michael Elphick being interviewed

SOMETHING OLD, SOMETHING NEW EPISODE 7

DIRECTED BY Oliver Horsbrugh
ORIGINAL AIR DATE: May 18, 1980

CAST

Alan Dobie.......Detective Sergeant Cribb
William Simons......Constable Thackeray
Charlotte Mitchell.................Mrs. Winter
Geoffrey Bayldon.......Uncle Ezra Winter
Sally Osborne...................Daphne Winter
Ivor Salter......................................Sexton
Arthur Hewlett...................Henry Russell
George Waring........................Dr. Burden
William Abney................................Vicar
Alison Glennie...................Denise Winter
Marjorie Sudell.............Woman On Train

Alan Dobie

William Simons

Charlotte Mitchell

Geoffrey Bayldon

Sally Osborne

Ivor Salter

Arthur Hewlett

George Waring

William Abney

Alison Glennie

Marjorie Sudell

Curate

Little Boy

Patient

When Cribb notices Thackery getting his suit pressed, he discovers that Thackeray is to be the best man at the wedding of a friend of his father, elderly Henry Russell who is marrying a woman nearly fifty years his junior.

Geoffrey Bayldon, Ivor Salter

Sally Osborne, Arthur Hewlett

Charlotte Mitchell, William Simons

Alan Dobie, Geoffrey Bayldon, William Simons

The vicar is suspicious and, when Cribb investigates, it is discovered that both the bride and her sister have been married before to men very much their senior who died soon after the weddings.

A poisonous plant in the garden arouses Cribb's suspicions. When Thackeray tells Cribb that Henry has suffered a heart attack, the two policemen decide to pay a visit.

Alan Dobie, William Simons

Little Boy and Marjorie Sudell

Arthur Hewlett, William Simons, Alan Dobie

William Simons & Arthur Hewlett

The heart attack had come after eating some mutton prepared by his new wife's mother. Couple that with the fact that Henry was persuaded to draw up a will, Cribb really becomes interested.

After visiting Henry's doctor and a vicar who tells a story of a May-December marriage, Cribb is now certain the women are out to poison Henry.

TV Poster

Alison Glennie, Charlotte Mitchell

Alan Dobie, William Abney

Alan Dobie in the church

Cribb confronts Mrs. Winter and her daughters directly, telling them that if anything happens to Henry, they will begin exhumations on the former elderly victims.

Cribb grabs a bowl of soup meant for Henry, which is taken from him and thrown out the window. Now he knows. He says he, the police, and the doctor all know-so they better take really good care of Henry!

Charlotte Mitchell, Alan Dobie, Alison Glennie

Arthur Hewlett, Alan Dobie, Sally Osborne

Geoffrey Bayldon as the Reverend

A CASE OF SPIRITS EPISODE 8

DIRECTED BY Bill Gilmour

ORIGINAL AIR DATE: May 25, 1980

CAST

Alan Dobie.......Detective Sergeant Cribb
Thorley Walters....Chief Inspector Jowett
William Simons......Constable Thackeray
Clive Swift.............................Dr. Probert
Judy Cornwell.......................Miss Crush
Georgine Anderson........Winifred Probert
Michael Barrington.......Professor Quayle
Christopher Hancock.......Mr. Strathmore
Mick Ford.............................Peter Brand
Emma Jacobs......................Alice Probert
David Neville.......................Captain Nye
John Warner........................Dr. Benjamin
Geoffrey Larder.........................Mr. Cage

Alan Dobie

Thorley Walters

William Simons

Clive Swift

Judy Cornwell

Georgine Anderson

Michael Barrington

Christopher Hancock

Mick Ford

Emma Jacobs

David Neville

John Warner

Geoffrey Larder

Inspector Jowett brings Cribb and Thackery to an art academy, where he points to a picture, telling them that it has already been stolen. The stolen one was in fact a nearly identical picture painted by the same artist.

Thorley Walters as the Inspector

Alan Dobie & William Simons

Thorley Walters, William Simons, Alan Dobie

Clive Swift, Alan Dobie

Two robberies at the homes of patrons of a medium holding séances in their houses seems rather more than coincidence but Jowett belongs to a group investigating the honesty of the medium.

The medium, young Peter Brand, is wired electrically to a bell which will ring if he moves in such a way that suggests trickery. Unfortunately the wiring explodes and he is killed.

Geoffrey Larder, John Warner

Georgine Anderson, Michael Barrington

Mick Ford, Alan Dobie

Thackeray and Cribb in the audience

Cribb is called to investigate a death that was certainly not perpetrated by somebody from the spirit world. Cribb determines that Professor Quayle is guilty of larceny.

William Simons, Alan Dobie

Michael Barrington, Alan Dobie

Michael Barrington shows some pictures

But Mrs. Probert tells Cribb that Quayle was there at her invitation. Cribb drops the charges. Back at the Probert home, Cribb has another seance with all those who were present when Brand died.

Television Poster

Cribb says that it was years of hope that provoked a betrayal, which ultimately led to the killing of Brand-which was not premeditated. The killer says that if Brand was a genuine medium, he would not have touched the handkerchief, which caused his death.

William Simons, Alan Dobie

William Simons, Alan Dobie

Alan Dobie as Sergeant Cribb

MAD HATTER'S HOLIDAY EPISODE 9

DIRECTED BY June Wyndham-Davies
ORIGINAL AIR DATE: March 29, 1981

CAST

Alan Dobie.......Detective Sergeant Cribb
William Simons......Constable Thackeray
David Waller.........Chief Inspector Jowett
Derek Fowlds..................Albert Moscrop
Fenella Fielding................Zena Prothero
Conrad Phillips.....................Dr. Prothero
Kevin Brennan.............Inspector Murphy
George Lee.................Constable Murphy
Adam Richardson...............Guy Prothero
Kate Lock.....................................Bridget

Alan Dobie

William Simons

David Waller

Derek Fowlds

Fenella Fielding

Conrad Phillips

Kevin Brennan

George Lee

Adam Richardson

Kate Lock

Parts of a dismembered female corpse have turned up in Brighton and Cribb and Thackeray are sent to investigate. They are approached by Albert Moscrop, a hat-maker taking a holiday in the resort.

William Simons as Constable Thackeray

Examination of a clue

He has binoculars and a telescope which he uses to observe people and is something of a voyeur. He tells Cribb how he met the charming but nervous Zena Prothero, the second wife of a rather surly doctor.

Alan Dobie, Kevin Brennan, William Simons

Fenella Fielding on horseback

Alan Dobie & Derek Fowlds

Looks like I may lose my hat!

Mr. Prothero is on holiday with their son Guy. Moscrop believes that Zena was killed by her husband and certainly some anatomical knowledge was displayed in the cutting of the body.

But was Prothero the killer? And is Zena the victim? Moscrop plays detective and keeps an eye on the Prothero home. Constable Thackeray finds a clue that looks like it points to Prothero.

Alan Dobie, Derek Fowlds

Alan Dobie, Derek Fowlds

Meanwhile Moscrop sees Mrs. Prothero riding a horse; he tells Cribb, who is not surprised. On horseback, Cribb confronts her. He says the dismembered woman was Bridget, servant to Mrs. Moscrop.

Fenella Fielding, Derek Fowlds

Derek Fowlds, Fenella Fielding

Fenella Fielding, Alan Dobie

Alan Dobie, William Simons

Alan Dobie as Sergeant Cribb

After the death of Prothero's son, Cribb reckons the young man may have been injected with some sort of poison. Prothero says that extreeme remedies are needed for extreme diseases. Cribb knows what happened and why, but says he can never prove it in a court of law.

Derek Fowlds, Kate Lock

Derek Fowlds, Alan Dobie

THE LAST TRUMPET EPISODE 10

DIRECTED BY Brian Mills
ORIGINAL AIR DATE: April 5, 1981

CAST

Alan Dobie.......Detective Sergeant Cribb
William Simons......Constable Thackeray
David Waller.........Chief Inspector Jowett
Joyce Carey.....................Mrs. Pennycock
Geoffrey Keen..............Abraham Bartlett
Barry Jackson....................Matthew Scott
Garrick Hagon..............William Newman
Tony Steedman.............Sebastian Napier
Mary Larkin.................................Louise
Lee Whitlock...............................Bobby
Norman Mills................Turnstile Keeper
Alfie Curtis...............................Landlord
John de Frates.....................Wine Vintner

Alan Dobie

William Simons

David Waller

Joyce Carey

Geoffrey Keen

Barry Jackson

Garrick Hagon

Tony Steedman

Mary Larkin

Lee Whitlock

Norman Mills

Alfie Curtis

Flower Seller Zoo Patron 1 Zoo Patron 2

The police are guarding Jumbo, the elephant that is one of the prime attractions at the London Zoo, because certain people are up in arms about his being sold to American showman P. T. Barnum and scheduled to be shipped across the Atlantic.

Geoffrey Keen as Abraham Bartlett

TV Poster

Alan Dobie and Jumbo

Jumbo has occasional attacks of musth, a common feature in elephants and camels that lead them towards the baser instincts, which makes him periodically unsafe for giving visitors rides around the zoo.

Eccentric old Mrs. Pennycock leads a protest against the exporting of the elephant, writing songs about Jumbo to swell her cause. She visits the head of the zoo, Abraham Bartlett, with a petition to keep Jumbo.

Joyce Carey, Geoffrey Keen

Thackeray in front of Jumbo's cage

Barry Jackson as Jumbo's trainer

William Simons, Alan Dobie, Geoffrey Keen

When she leaves, Jowett and Thackeray arrive. They tell Bartlett they are taking every precaution to safeguard the elephant. Back at her home, Mrs. Pennycock has been given an anonymous bottle of wine, left on her doorstep.

Tony Steedman, Mary Larkin

David Waller at the zoo gate

Sergeant Cribb holds a clue

Entrance to the zoo

David Waller enjoys a glass of wine

When she drinks it, she dies from poison. Could the killer have been Barnum's representative or Jumbo's keeper, both of whom were her opponents and who will soon be leaving the country with Jumbo?

But it turns out the killer, who expected a legacy from the old lady, winds up with nothing, as Mrs. Pennycock's lawyer had embezzled all her funds away!

Joyce Carey with her pamphlets

William Simons, David Waller

Alan Dobie as Sergeant Cribb

THE HAND THAT ROCKS THE CRADLE EPISODE 11

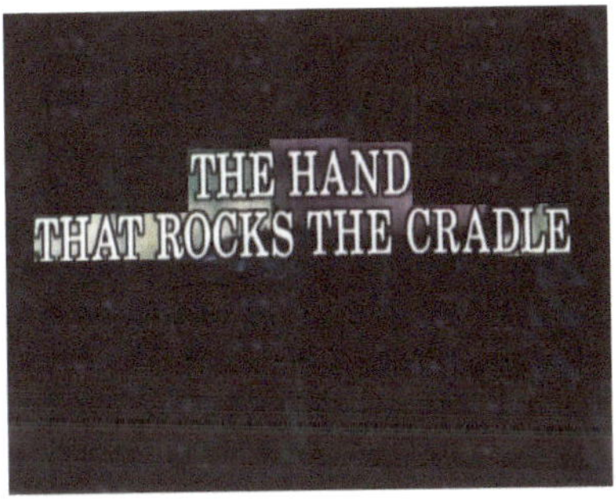

DIRECTED BY George Spenton-Foster
ORIGINAL AIR DATE: April 12, 1981

CAST

Alan Dobie.......Detective Sergeant Cribb
David Waller.........Chief Inspector Jowett
William Simons......Constable Thackeray
Rosalie Crutchley...............Mrs. Innocent
Jessica Spencer.................Queen Victoria
Timothy Carlton..Superintendent Wilmot
Aubrey Woods............Lord Caspar-Jones
Jane Sherwin....................Lady Mortimer
Irene Richard................Princess Beatrice
Scott Fredericks...................Prince Henry
Nicholas Day..........................Igor Ozolin
Sarah Neville.........................Jane Temple
Virginia Denham...................Nurse Grant
Timothy Stark.............Huw Caspar-Jones
Francesca Gerard....Gwyneth Caspar-Jones

Alan Dobie

David Waller

William Simons

Rosalie Crutchley

Jessica Spencer

Timothy Carlton

Aubrey Woods

Jane Sherwin

Irene Richard

Scott Fredericks

Nicholas Day

Sarah Neville

Virginia Denham

Timothy Stark

Francesca Gerard

At Windsor Castle's coach house late at night, a mysterious hand is seen applying what looks like grease to the royal pram.

Television Poster

Scott Fredericks as Prince Henry

Jessica Spencer as Queen Victoria

Jessica Spencer, Irene Richard

William Simons with David Waller et al

After the fortunately empty pram accidentally rolls away and nearly collides with the monarch, the infant's nursemaid is sacked, creating a vacancy.

The child's parents want young, progressive Miss Temple but the Queen is in favour of her daughter's old nurse, Mrs. Innocent, an austere, gin-swigging old dragon.

Lovely view of the Royal Garden

Francesca Gerard, Timothy Stark

Irene Richard, Scott Fredericks

Alan Dobie, William Simons

The child's father Prince Henry asks Cribb to investigate Mrs. Innocent, currently employed in caring for the two children of an eccentric composer, for proof of unsuitability through senility.

Cribb investigates and finds that the pram was sabotaged in order to create a vacancy close to the Crown. The two candidates for the nursemaid position come under suspicion.

Alan Dobie, William Simons

Alan Dobie, David Waller

Jowett displays the mugs

Timothy Carlton, Alan Dobie

Thackeray is keeping an eye on Mrs. Innocent; he follows her into a woman's suffragette meeting, where the women attack him and take his trousers. He returns to the office wearing a Union Jack!

Cribb discovers that the perambulator had been greased and altered; he tells Superintendent Wilmot that this is part of an anarchist plot. After arresting those involved, Cribb receives a token of gratitude from the Queen-a scarf knitted by Mrs. Innocent.

Uh-oh! Royal pram crashed in the water

Rosalie Crutchley knitting

THE CHOIR THAT WOULDN'T SING EPISODE 12

DIRECTED BY Mary McMurray
ORIGINAL AIR DATE: April 19, 1981

CAST

Alan Dobie.......Detective Sergeant Cribb
William Simons......Constable Thackeray
David Waller.........Chief Inspector Jowett
Elizabeth Spriggs.................Mrs. Gurney
Ben Aris........................Captain Allbright
Barry McGinn..........................Mr. Jessop
Gilbert Wynne.....................Albert Harris
Douglas Milvain.......................Mr. Wood
David Jackson....................Henry Willing
Alan Downer........................Joshua Pugh
Jeremy Clay.......................Walter Fenner
Moir Leslie.....................Bernice Dawson
Enn Reitel.............................Mr. Strange
David John Duffy, Sean Martin, Paul Moloney, Mark Robinson......Choir Boys

Alan Dobie

William Simons

David Waller

Elizabeth Spriggs

Ben Aris

Barry McGinn

Gilbert Wynne

Douglas Milvain

David Jackson

Alan Downer

Jeremy Clay

Moir Leslie

Enn Reitel

Sergeant

Cribb and Thackeray go to the country to investigate the death of unpopular Colonel Dawson who died as he was about to change his will in favour of birds' egg collectors, and his regiment.

William Simons, Elizabeth Spriggs, Alan Dobie

Sergeant giving a salute

Douglas Milvain, David Jackson

Alan Dobie, David Jackson

The colonel was running through the woods at night being chased by an unknown assailant, and fell into a gravel pit. He sang in the local choir, but the other members did not like him.

They claim to have been at choir practice but there are inconsistencies in their stories which lead Cribb to suspect a conspiracy. When Thackeray questions them, they all say different things-even to the songs and hymns that were sung.

A smiling David Waller

William Simons, Alan Dobie

Ben Aris, Alan Dobie

Moir Leslie, Elizabeth Spriggs

Cribb visits the regiment, where Captain Allbright says that the colonel would never have killed himself. Cribb also learns Dawson had a son, Harry, who died of cholera.

Thackeray watches a large trunk-or coffin-being delivered to a house, just before he gets hit over the head from behind. After he recovers, Cribb is on the scene and discovers Albert Harris delivered it.

David Jackson, Jeremy Clay

Pallbearers at the funeral

William Simons in the pit

William Simons, Barry McGinn

Barry McGinn, William Simons

It transpires that Harry married a woman shortly before he died; his father was about to change his will, but was killed before he could sign the new one.

When Dawson refused to change the will, the entire town was outraged. Cribb says he will let Jowett decide the outcome-and the Chief Inspector decides Dawson's death was an accident.

William Simons, David Waller

Local police help Sergeant Cribb

MURDER OLD BOY? EPISODE 13

DIRECTED BY George Spenton-Foster
ORIGINAL AIR DATE: May 3, 1981

CAST

Alan Dobie.......Detective Sergeant Cribb
David Waller.........Chief Inspector Jowett
William Simons......Constable Thackeray
John Carson..................Russell Haygarth
Edgar Wreford.................Montague Penn
Eric Dodson.........................James Archer
John Bryans..........................Dr. Partridge
Terence Edmond...................Headmaster
Petra Davies.................................Matron

Alan Dobie

David Waller

William Simons

John Carson

Edgar Wreford

Eric Dodson

John Bryans

Terence Edmond

Petra Davies

Russell Haygarth comes to Scotland Yard seeking his old school friend Inspector Jowett - he finds Cribb, whom he initially mistakes for Jowett. Cribb directs him to the correct office.

Haygarth find Jowett and invites him to attend a reunion weekend; Jowett is reluctant at first, but Haygarth says there will only be a handful of people, specifically invited. Jowett decides to go.

Eric Dodson, Edgar Wreford, David Waller, John Bryans

Alan Dobie, William Simons, David Waller

David Waller, Petra Davies

William Simons, Alan Dobie

He arrives at the Petersham Boarding School for Boys, where he is greeted by some of his former classmates, who assault him with pillows. Jowett considers this behaviour childish.

Discovering that Haygarth is a convicted swindler, Cribb and Thackeray travel to warn Jowett and find that Haygarth is hoping to relieve the company of their money for a supposed donation to the school.

David Waller as Chief Inspector Jowett

David Waller arrives for the reunion

Haygarth visits the Chief Inspector

David Waller, John Bryans, Eric Dodson

That night he is found hanged; is it murder or suicide? James Archer confesses that Haygarth seduced his wife and, given that none of the eminent men are what they seem, they are all suspect.

The former schoolmates are concerned that news of the death will create adverse publicity for the school. Matron, who was on the way to Haygarth with some cocoa, is also questioned by Cribb.

John Carson as Russell Haygarth

Edgar Wreford, John Bryans

John Carson, William Simons

Eric Dodson, John Bryans, Edgar Wreford

Eric Dodson as James Archer

Cribb deduces the killer was hiding in the room when Matron came in; when she left to get help, he escaped. Cribb discovers that the headmaster's mother had been swindled years before by Haygarth. She lost her home and her life savings.

He strangled Haygarth, then strung him up and wrote a suicide note. He thought the "old boys" would rally behind him, but they all say no. "We don't remain schoolboys forever," Jowett tells him

John Bryans, Edgar Wreford, David Waller, Eric Dodson

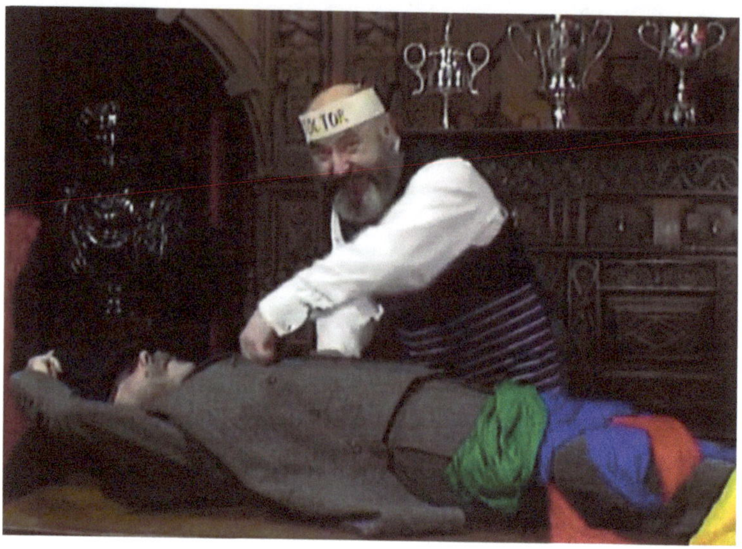

The old boys put on a skit

INVITATION TO A DYNAMITE PARTY EPISODE 14

DIRECTED BY Alan Grint

ORIGINAL AIR DATE: May 10, 1981

CAST

Alan Dobie.......Detective Sergeant Cribb
David Waller.........Chief Inspector Jowett
William Simons......Constable Thackeray
Charles Keating.............................Devlin
James Taylor.....................Colonel Martin
Antony Scott................................Malone
David Sterne...................................Carter
Jeanne Crowley.........Rossanna McGee
Tony Scannell................................Millar
Derry Power...................................Carse
Tommy Brierley............................McGee
Colin Bean.......................................P.C.
Ian Keith.....................................Officer
Eileen Fletcher................................Maid

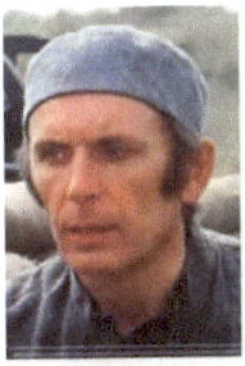
Alan Dobie

David Waller

William Simons

Charles Keating

James Taylor

Antony Scott

David Sterne

Jeanne Crowley

Tony Scannell

Derry Power

Tommy Brierley

Colin Bean

Ian Keith

Fenians intent on the independence of Ireland from Britain are perpetrating a number of bomb attacks around London, including at Scotland Yard.

James Taylor, David Waller

Charles Keating, Alan Dobie

David Waller as Chief Inspector Jowett

Television Poster

Cribb is sent on a course in the art of bomb-making and poses as an Irishman sympathetic to the Irish Republican Brotherhood in order to get to the heart of the society.

Jeanne Crowley as Rossanna McGee

Charles Keating, Rossanna McGee

Jowett tells Cribb all about the dynamite conspiracy. It seems that a policeman may be involved; Jowett tells Cribb that Constable Thackeray has fallen under suspicion.

Derry Power, Tony Scannel

Derry Power, Tony Scannel

William Simons, Alan Dobie

Alan Dobie, Jeananne Crowley

Certain members of the brotherhood get hold of Cribb to join them on a submarine where they want him to blow up a brand new British battle-ship to prove his allegiance to the cause.

So Cribb makes two bombs, but he makes sure neither one will work; the submarine runs itself aground several miles away without having been blown up.

Alan Dobie, Charles Keating

Derry Power, Tony Scannel

Alan Dobie as Sergeant Cribb

Alan Dobie, David Waller

Ship is the target for destruction

Jowett commends Cribb and also tells him that Constable Thackeray is a very good policeman. Apparently the Commissioner was so pleased with Cribb, he is sending the sergeant on a complete demolition course at Woolwich Arsenal.

Milton Keynes UK
Ingram Content Group UK Ltd.
UKHW050143160124
436103UK00001B/1

9781087893204